Assertiveness: Get What You Want Without Being Pushy

Written by Cal LeMon
Edited by National Press Publications

NATIONAL PRESS PUBLICATIONS
A Division of Rockhurst College Continuing Education Center, Inc.
6901 West 63rd Street • P.O. Box 2949 • Shawnee Mission, Kansas 66201-1349
1-800-258-7246 • 1-913-432-7757

National Seminars endorses non-sexist language. However, in an effort to make this handbook clear, consistent and easy to read, we've used the generic "he" when referring to both males and females throughout. The copy is not intended to be sexist.

Printed in the United States of America

10

ISBN 1-55852-033-3

Table of Contents

1
THE ASSERTIVE CHOICE

Today you made a series of important choices.

You chose a particular color dress, the route to and from work, sugar or artificial sweetener in your coffee, NBC or CNN for the evening news, to floss or not to floss, and what time the alarm will go off tomorrow morning.

And, you made another significant choice today. You decided, not one but several times, who you were going to be. This choice was not about becoming a Walter Mitty, a Miss America or a Dr. Jekyll. Rather, the decision was what type of person you would be when other people tried to squeeze you into their agenda.

Specifically, after the alarm went off, did someone in your house demand to use the bathroom before you thought your time was up? Did your boss insist you rewrite a report in the next 48 hours? Did a waiter take your plate before you were finished eating lunch?

There is no way to avoid conflict. It is woven into the fabric of everyday life. If you rub shoulders with people, you can also count on knocking heads as well.

Since conflict is inevitable, it is important that we decide what type of person we will be when "push comes to shove." Basically, there are three types of behavior we can choose when conflict arises. We can be aggressive, passive or assertive.

The Aggressive Person

Built into each of us is the animal instinct called "fight or flight." When we are threatened, we have instinctive responses. We can "fight" by punching someone's lights out or verbally go right for his jugular with words we know will hurt. Or we can choose "flight" which usually involves turning on our heels and running as fast as we can.

The aggressive person is someone who chooses, on a regular basis, to fight. His strategy is best defined as "one-upmanship."

At the core of the aggressive person is a deep fear of being engulfed or swallowed up by someone else. Probably there is history of being victimized by someone very "big." The big person could have been taller, louder, smarter, prettier, funnier or richer. To make sure that big people don't get the upper hand, the aggressive person makes it his priority to always be "bigger."

Aggressive behavior may include physically invading some-one's space, making obscene gestures or regularly issuing ultimatums.

To determine if you have an aggressive behavior style, answer "yes" or "no" to the following statements:

1. When making a point, I often point my finger at people.

2. I stare at people I don't like.

3. When I'm angry, I have been known to scream.

4. When walking with someone down a hall, I usually am one step ahead.

5. I cannot stand to wait for my order at a fast-food restaurant.

6. I am very good at the "put-down."

7. I often answer for other people.

8. When I am in a group, the conversation really starts rolling.

9. I really like the saying, "To err is human, to forgive is not part of my job description."

10. People have told me they are afraid of me.

If you answered "yes" to six or more of the above statements, aggressive behavior may be the norm in your relationships.

You may be like Jeff. Jeff is a middle manager anxious to move "up the ladder" by impressing his boss with his ability to get the task done. Here is Jeff in the weekly staff meeting where a dismal sales report has just been distributed. Jeff's department has come under criticism. Another manager points his finger at Jeff across the conference table.

Manager: "Jeff, we need your help to increase productivity."

Jeff: (Rising from his chair while leaning forward with both hands on the table.) "What a joke. You don't want my help. You are just looking for someone to blame this mess on. Well, (shaking his fist in the air) I'm not going to be your fall guy, pal! (Screaming.) You can't get to me you...you...you wimp!"

Here is a classic aggressive response. Notice Jeff's physical attempt to intimidate by standing and leaning over the table. Also, Jeff defends himself against the criticism by getting "bigger" with put-downs and name-calling.

Jeff, and every other aggressive person, has a mortal fear of giving up control. If Jeff gives up control, he becomes controlled by others. The aggressive person sees every challenge as a potential personal attack to make him "kneel and knuckle." Once the ranting and raving is complete, the aggressor is confident that, with diligence, he can keep others from infringing on his personal rights.

The Passive Person

Some favorite aphorisms of the passive person are "don't rock the boat," "let sleeping dogs lie" and "don't make waves." Passivity is not always bad. On a lazy Saturday morning after a hard week at work, being passive can be your body's way of saying, "I need a break."

But passive responses, especially in a conflict situation, can signal an unwillingness to be an adult. Passivity can complicate adult communication by confusing the real message with silence and double-meanings.

You might say, "Sometimes I don't want to deal with issues between myself and others." You have the right to say that. But, if that behavior goes on for any length of time, it becomes an habitual attempt at avoidance which usually is destructive to relationships.

More specifically, if we "clam up" when confronted, passive-aggressive behavior becomes the norm. Passive-aggressive behavior is characterized by acting out with our bodies what our insides really want to say.

For example, if you have aggressive feelings toward your boss but are afraid to verbally confront him because of the threat of being fired, you may, unconsciously, begin arriving a few minutes late to work every day. With this passive-aggressive behavior, you are acting out the conflict without ever talking about it. Walking in three to five minutes late will drive this person crazy without jeopardizing your job.

Passive-aggressive behavior is the worst kind of passivity. As a matter of fact, it really is not passive at all. It is an underground way of letting others know your real feelings without taking responsibility for those feelings.

If you would like to find out if you have some passive tendencies, count the number of "yes" responses to the following statements:

1. I often talk with my hand over my mouth.

2. One of the things I say a lot is, "Nothing, I'm just thinking."

3. When meeting someone for the first time, I'm not comfortable making eye contact.

4. I usually slump while sitting.

5. I think whining drives people crazy.

6. I usually ask permission to use the restroom when I'm in a staff meeting.

7. When I say, "I'm angry," I always smile.

8. I apologized for the weather when relatives recently visited my home.

9. I do not like arguments.

10. A lot of people take advantage of me.

If you answered "yes" to six or more, you may have developed some passive behavior when dealing with conflict.

Let's go back to Jeff for a minute. It is the same conference room and the same staff meeting. Notice the differences between an aggressive and a passive Jeff.

Manager: "Jeff, we need your help to increase productivity."

Jeff: "You guys are always on my back about something. Go ahead, what's the big deal today? I'm ready to take it on the chin again. (Sigh) This happens at every staff meeting."

The marks of passivity are unmistakable. First, Jeff has cast himself in the lead role of "Martyr for a Day." When the passive person sees himself as the "underdog," people can be easily manipulated. Power for Jeff is that he is powerless. He likes that position because it guarantees he will get what he cannot get through adult confrontation.

Second, Jeff used the word "always." This is an inclusive term. It means that from the beginning of Jeff's history with these people, they have been "out to get him." This establishes Jeff as a victim. For the victim, life is an endless tale of others trying to take advantage of him.

If someone constantly sees himself as a victim, he can justify his anti-social behavior. The aloneness, solitary coffee breaks and never showing up at the annual Christmas party are all expected responses from the victim. Getting "too close" to others, the victim believes, will always end with him getting the leftovers of any relationship.

The Assertive Person

The assertive person is far different from either the aggressive or passive personality. The assertive person is willing to take responsibility for his actions. There is no game-playing in assertiveness. When someone asserts himself, he has made the decision to be an adult.

There are four major components to assertiveness:

1. The assertive person clearly represents what he is thinking and feeling.

2. There is no apology for expressing emotions and thoughts.

3. The assertive person refuses to be manipulated by false guilt (guilt instilled by someone else) when communicating.

4. Others' rights are never sacrificed to get one's own way.

Assertiveness begins with the assumption that each human being is given rights that do not depend on performance or position. That idea often runs counter to what we have been taught since early childhood.

The first component assumes that all of us have a "right" to express ourselves. Who gives us that right? We assume that "rights" are earned. You only have the right to vote if you are a good citizen. You have the right to drive a car if you obey the traffic laws. And we have the right to success if we work hard.

Most "rights" are conditional. We achieve the right if the "if clause" is met. Yes, you will keep your license if you obey the laws; and yes, you may have success if you work hard. But there are some "rights" (life, liberty, pursuit of happiness) that are yours regardless of your title, how much money you earn or any other conditions. Your ability to assert yourself is one of those rights.

You can see assertiveness in the first six months of life. When a baby wants food, warmth or a dry diaper, he is not going to try aggressiveness or passivity. He will assert himself! As a baby grows up, he learns how to manipulate through power or weakness to get what he wants. Somewhere along the way, he may be taught that assertiveness means being "pushy."

Below you will find the assertive person's "Bill of Rights." These assumptions provide the basis for an understanding of assertiveness.

The Rights of the Assertive Person

1. You have the right to be human and take full responsibility for your decisions and actions.

2. You have the right to be wrong.

3. You have the right to tell others what you are thinking and feeling.

4. You have the right to change your mind.

5. You have the right to stand in judgment of your thoughts and actions.

6. You have the right to express yourself without intimidation or guilt.

7. You have the right not to accept responsibility for others.

These rights do not have to be fought for or proved. They are part of your basic human rights.

You are saying right now, "Tell that to my boss or spouse." No, you tell them. That's the purpose of this book. In these pages, you will learn the communication skills necessary to tell someone you have basic assertive rights.

Complete the exercise below to decide if you already are using some of these rights. You may be surprised how effective you already are as an assertive communicator. How many of these statements get a "yes" response from you?

1. I can say "no" without feeling guilty.

2. I have a reputation for being a good listener.

3. I like the saying, "Try, they can only say no."

4. In the last year, I have not lost control of my emotions.

5. When I think of annual performance reviews, I don't get nervous.

6. I usually make mistakes and will make more.

7. I like to try new restaurants.

8. It is OK to go out "Dutch treat."

9. I fall asleep easily.

10. I am content with my life.

If you answered "yes" to six or more, you probably are an assertive person. You may want to go back and compare the other inventories given for the aggressive and passive person. What is the major difference?

The answer to this question should be apparent. The assertive person doesn't try to bully or whine his way through life to get what he wants. Assertiveness does not guarantee you will get what you want. However, it does give you the peace of mind that comes with knowing you have been honest with yourself and those around you.

Let's visit Jeff again. In the following dialogue, you will see a remarkable transformation from the patronizing "parent" and the whimpering "child" to the assertive "adult."

Manager: "Jeff, we need your help to increase productivity."

Jeff: "I know there are problems in my department. The facts tell the tale. Do you have suggestions for me?"

The threat is gone. Even though the manager may have been trying to intimidate Jeff, this assertive person takes responsibility just for himself. Jeff's response is filled with genuine self-confidence.

At the heart of assertiveness is the confidence that, even though no one else may give approval, the final approval comes from within. This is not arrogance — this is assertiveness.

For Your Review

In this chapter we learned the basics of assertiveness as we contrasted an assertive person with one who is aggressive and one who is passive. We choose one of these three behaviors daily when faced with interpersonal relationships that involve conflict.

To determine if you have made the distinction between these three behaviors, read each of the following statements and decide if it is an assertive, aggressive or passive response.

1. "You are right, the mistakes on this month's report are my fault."

2. "Even though I cannot remember saying that, I'm sure you are right."

3. "This report reminds me of you—worthless!"

4. "I understand what you are asking for, but I do not have time to help you right now."

5. "You claim you didn't know. Come on, I wasn't born yesterday!"

(1. Assertive 2. Passive 3. Aggressive 4. Assertive 5. Aggressive)

2

STEPS TO BECOMING
AN ASSERTIVE PERSON

Assertiveness is not something you do — assertiveness is who you are.

In the past few years, the American public has been bombarded with slogans like "You are what you eat" and "You are what you wear." So a lot of us have been eating bales of alfalfa sprouts and draping our bodies in designer labels.

But another saying which has stood the test of time and always proved true is "You are what you think." What we tell ourselves we can do, we usually do.

The best example of this principle is a human running a mile in less than four minutes. For hundreds of years, people believed it was physiologically impossible for anyone to run a mile in less than four minutes.

The pages of history are filled with some very creative attempts at breaking the four-minute mile. Ancient Greeks released lions to chase Olympic runners as an incentive to run faster. Often the Greeks only succeeded in reducing the field of contestants while increasing smiles on the faces of the lions.

Then on May 6, 1954, an Englishman named Roger Bannister did the impossible. Word spread around the world that the four-minute mile was shattered. What is astonishing is that same year 37 other people ran the mile in under four minutes. In 1955, over 300 athletes also broke the four-minute barrier.

Did the bodies of runners suddenly become stronger in 1954? Obviously, the answer is no. What changed were the possibilities in an athlete's mind.

How we view ourselves will shape our behavior both positively and negatively. If we can push back the walls of our minds, we can achieve that promotion, make that sale, chip in that nine-iron shot or write that book.

Becoming an assertive person begins with our minds. If we are not comfortable with how we view ourselves, then assertiveness is just another manipulative game to play. Within the foundation of assertiveness is a fundamental assumption — all assertive people like themselves.

Developing Your Self-Image

Liking yourself does not happen overnight. Throughout life, our self-image has been shaped by three developmental stages:

1. Self-awareness.

2. Self-esteem.

3. Self-confidence.

In the first stage, self-awareness, we received some powerful messages about who we are from our parents, our peers and those quiet conversations we had with ourselves.

What messages did you get from your parents about who you are? Take a few minutes to carefully read the list of expressions which follow. Which collection of words did you hear most often as a child?

1. "Children should be seen and not heard."

2. "You can do it!"

3. "Don't you ever think before you do something?"

4. "Just do your best — that is always good enough for us."

5. "Wait until your father gets home!"

6. "We love you."

7. "How could you do something like this after all we have done for you?"

8. "We don't expect you to be perfect."

9. "You are a bad boy/girl."

10. "Whatever you decide, we will support you."

If you heard more odd numbered statements than even numbered ones, it could be you received negative messages about who you are as a person. As an adult, can you still hear those words? Isn't it true that other adults in your life can be stand-in parents? Have you ever thought a boss sounded remarkably like your mother or father?

These childhood messages have been imprinted on our memories. The negativity of being "bad" or "fat" or "dumb" may drag behind us for a lifetime like tin cans tied to a honeymooner's car.

Dr. Margaret Mahler, a noted child psychologist, said the messages we receive in the first three years of life are the loudest voices in our adult minds. As a matter of fact, according to Dr. Mahler, all of life after age three is only practice of what we learned about ourselves in those short 36 months!

The first step to freedom from this negative childhood imprinting is to assert that you are not "bad." This assertion requires courage — the courage to judge yourself without parental approval. This is the moment when you are free to become an adult.

The adult is able to love, respect and admire his parents without becoming engulfed by their parental evaluations and expectations. When this process is complete, the separation anxiety of emotionally leaving "home" is finally over.

The second source of self-awareness is the messages sent by other adults. In other words, "What do people say about me?" To find out what those messages may be, mentally complete the statements below.

1. When I leave a room of friends, they may say, "He is really a _____."

2. On my annual performance reviews, the word I see most often is _____.

3. When there is conflict at work, my co-workers usually ask me to _____.

4. At the annual Christmas party, I am generally seen as:
   a. the "party animal"
   b. the "wall flower"
   c. the "Scrooge"
   d. other _____

5. If I were unexpectedly promoted tomorrow, my co-workers would say, "He _____."

Maybe some of those responses surprised you. Much of the information that shapes how we see ourselves is supplied by people around us.

There are basically two ways we respond to those closest to us. First, we are *reflective,* meaning we fill the roles people cast for us. For example, if others keep telling you that you are a "barrel of laughs," do you feel it is your responsibility to make every coffee break conversation a scene from "Saturday Night Live"?

Second, we can be *oppositional.* Even though co-workers tell you that you have a heart as big as Mother Teresa, do you occasionally act out Rambo just to prove that you have another side?

Most of the time we bend over backwards to be reflective.
The final source of our self-awareness is that moment when
we look in the mirror and have those personal conversations
with the person we know best.

To help define who you see in the mirror, find the words in
the list below that describe the real you.

Accepting	Impulsive	Quiet
Adaptive	Innovative	Realistic
Belligerent	Joyful	Reflective
Bold	Judgmental	Rigid
Careless	Kind	Sarcastic
Clever	Knowledgeable	Serious
Dependable	Loving	Sociable
Domineering	Logical	Tactful
Effective	Manipulative	Tense
Energetic	Modest	Trusting
Fearful	Nervous	Uncertain
Foolish	Noisy	Warm
Free	Objective	Wishful
Friendly	Organized	Withdrawn
Gruff	Passive	Witty
Guilty	Perceptive	Worried
Happy	Quarrelsome	Wornout

You just labeled yourself. When you made the decision to
choose a certain word, you began to be more specific about how
you define your self-image. Are the words you picked different
from the words your parents or friends would have used?

Here is a homework assignment in assertive communication.
If you have just had a revelation, a moment when you have
discovered something about yourself, why not write a letter to a
parent or friend and let them know who you really are.

Once you have an accurate picture of yourself, you can move
to the second stage of developing an assertive self-image:
valuing yourself. This stage is also called self-esteem.

Valuing yourself is learned behavior — it does not come naturally.

Think of the punishment and reward system used in your childhood. When you were good you got a lollipop, an increase in your allowance or an extra hour watching television.

If you were bad, you may have been sent to bed (don't you wish you could be punished that way now!), received a spanking or been grounded.

When we give value to ourselves, we offer worth to both the good and bad in us. An assertive adult learns to make an honest list of strengths and weaknesses without denying either list.

Take a few moments right now to decide what are your strengths and weaknesses. After you have mentally compiled both lists, answer these important questions.

1. Which of the strengths do you reward?

2. Which of the weaknesses do you punish?

3. How do you punish yourself?

4. Which weakness could be a strength?

5. Which strength could be a weakness?

The end result of doing this exercise is to be able to say, "I am a strong and worthy person." An assertive person has a strong framework within himself which can support both the strengths and the weaknesses.

Punishment and reward are no longer the motivating forces in the assertive person. The assertive person has learned to approve of himself, not because he is perfect, but because he accepts his imperfections.

When self-awareness and self-esteem exist, you will be rewarded with self-confidence.

Self-confidence is not performed, it is projected. There is a big difference. Performing depends on other people. Projecting relies on yourself.

In psychological terms, the difference is an *extratensive* personality and an *intraversive* personality.

Extratensive personalities never get enough — of anything. These people are always in the middle of conversations at coffee break, staff meetings and meals. You can pick them out because activity usually revolves around them.

Some of the favorite statements used by an extratensive in a group will be:

- "Did you hear the one about..."

- "Let me tell you..."

- "They wouldn't get away with that if I were there."

- "I can't believe you..."

Notice how controlling those words are. The extratensive personality gets his value from others. In other words, these people only feel good when the grandstands are full and people are screaming for more.

The fatal flaw in the extratensive is he can never get enough attention. There is never enough laughter, enough slaps on the back, promotions, etc. This "never enough" issue often creates depression, leaving the extratensive very low after being very high. These people often berate themselves, privately, for not being good enough.

On the other side is the intraversive personality. He is open, verbal and quietly self-confident. This person wants to have close intimate relationships, but if someone doesn't offer "approval," for any reason, the intraversive is not destroyed.

Instead of looking for others to walk up and stamp "approved" on his forehead, the intraversive carries his own stamp. The ultimate source of approval, for the intraversive, is himself.

Obviously, self-confidence is the result of developing intraversive qualities.

Self-assertion is natural for the person who is naturally self-confident. On the other hand, becoming assertive can be another manipulative fad for the extratensive personality, who is deathly afraid of hearing silence in the grandstands.

The true test of whether or not assertiveness is a fad is when someone begins his assertive response with, "Since I am now an assertive person..." This condescending statement is intended to grab power in the conversation. The truly assertive person doesn't need to broadcast his assertiveness before he asserts himself. Only an extratensive personality tries this type of manipulation.

The process, then, of moving from self-awareness to self-esteem leads to self-confidence. Self-confidence has to exist in the mind before it is ever acted out with the body. Assertiveness begins with a healthy, self-confident person who has decided to like himself.

For Your Review

The opening line to this chapter summarizes the main idea of the pages you have just read, "Assertiveness is not something you do — assertiveness is who you are."

We have traced the process of moving from self-awareness to self-esteem to, finally, self-confidence. Self-confidence is the developmental stage in which the genuinely assertive person expresses himself. To review this process of moving toward self-confidence, complete the following sentences:

1. If I had to sum up in one sentence the main message I received about myself, as a child, it would be...

2. Today I see myself as having the potential to...

3. Learning to like who I am has been made easier because...

4. People around me do not understand that I am...

5. Becoming assertive is possible because I...

3

CONFRONTATION: THE FIRST STEP IN ASSERTIVE COMMUNICATION

Here he comes!

You know he will plow right into your privacy zone putting his face just two inches from your nose and start his usual tirade.

Not today!

Today you decide not to scream back (aggressive response) or silently bow your head (passive response). No, today you choose to be an assertive adult who will confront in response to confrontation.

Most of us fear confrontations. Our fear comes from memories of someone crushing us with his verbal or physical power. When we experience a confrontation, we often try to protect ourselves with one of these four "ego defense mechanisms":

1. Avoidance.

2. Repression.

3. Regression.

4. Blocking.

Avoidance is the practice of turning away from someone who threatens us. We avoid this person by taking a different hallway to our office, moving to the other side of the room, turning our back or even changing jobs.

Repression allows us to consciously push away unpleasant, recurring thoughts or memories. When a friend reminds you of a particularly awful moment in last week's staff meeting, you may use repression by saying, "I don't want to talk about it."

Regression is basically becoming a child again in order to defend yourself. Children are not expected to behave like adults. Sometimes we revert to childish responses to keep other adults from getting too close.

For example, have you ever confronted someone with a very difficult issue only to have him giggle like a teenager? The inappropriate laughter or feeble attempt to make a joke out of a sobering issue are characteristic of regression.

The final ego defense mechanism we possess is the strongest — *blocking*. When we block, our unconscious mind kicks in. If we suddenly face a severe emotional or physical trauma, our physical appearance may be described by others as "being in a daze." In fact, emotionally we cannot handle the sudden pain, so we involuntarily shut down our consciousness. The "daze" is an outward sign that our unconscious mind has just locked the door of our conscious.

Have you ever been fired? Have you been notified that someone close to you has died unexpectedly? Did a boss ever accuse you of lying in front of a group of co-workers?

If you answered yes to any of these questions, do you remember sliding into a daze? Those seconds of excruciating pain were probably followed by hours of emotional numbness as a result of blocking.

Even though our bodies and minds have some built-in escape hatches, we usually have choices about how we will respond to confrontation. Assertiveness is our best option.

Here he comes! Instead of avoiding, repressing or regressing (blocking is usually involuntary), you decide to confront this raging bull as an assertive adult. Before you say a word, notice the environment. Is there a crowd watching? The presence of other people is no accident. Crowds are part of your confronter's strategy.

When someone rants and raves, he usually needs an audience. There are two reasons why your raging bull needs a grandstand. First, he is intent on maintaining control. Control is temporarily achieved when he quickly fills a hallway or office with a booming voice or intimidating presence.

Second, he needs a crowd because crowds will control you. How? Crowds moderate responses. We know what we want to say to the person confronting us, but with an audience watching we have other concerns. What will these people think of me? Will I lose face with my peers? What will the conversation be like at lunch tomorrow?

Your attacker knows you are asking these questions. Notice that people who habitually make a scene only exhibit that behavior when there is an audience.

Assertiveness is not altered by either full or empty grandstands. The person who asserts himself is confident he must only take responsibility for himself.

You are free to judge your own decisions, so you can choose not to respond to this crowd manipulation. Obviously, your attacker wants to manipulate you into becoming aggressive (screaming back so he will be justified in raising the volume of his voice) or passive (you win "Wimp of the Year"). What this person is not counting on is your decision to be assertive.

Let him vent his anger until he takes a breath, slows down or turns blue. At that instant you say, "I will not deal with this issue right now; I will meet you at 1 p.m."

Notice in that statement there was no request for permission. Regardless of this person's title, privileged parking place or size of his weekly payroll check, you always have the right to buy time. If you are unable to emotionally or physically deal with someone (especially in front of a group), you can rewrite the setting without apology or guilt.

Let's look at your words a little closer. "...I will meet you at 1 p.m." gives you two advantages. First, you will share control in the next meeting because you initiated the appointment. Whoever begins a conversation usually directs the agenda.

Second, when you meet privately, the crowd is gone. You can now deal directly with the issues between the two of you without bouncing egos off applause meters.

If you have the choice of time and place for an assertive confrontation, you may want to make those decisions with the following information.

The Time for Confrontation

1. Avoid late-afternoon or evening encounters. Most people are exhausted at this time of day.

2. Meals are not productive times for conflict resolution. We are usually too busy trying to balance what looks good, sounds good and tastes good.

3. Do not plan conflict resolution immediately after staff meetings. It is too easy for both parties to drag the just-completed public agenda into the personal issues.

4. Set a time limit on the confrontation with a statement like, "I want to fully discuss this issue, but I have these other obligations." This preface sentence will give time parameters and extra incentive to work hard at resolving the issues.

5. Position yourself in the room so you can see a clock. Sneaking a look at your watch sends a nonverbal message, "Sorry, your time is up."

The Place for Confrontation

1. If you can, choose neutral territory (conference room, someone else's office). The neutrality of the location will keep each of you from positioning yourself for control.

2. If you are meeting in your office, do not sit behind your desk. Desks are often used as silent power manipulators.

3. If you are in the other person's office, avoid sitting in the middle of the room. When you are in the middle of the room directly in front of a large desk, you feel like you are being interrogated.

4. Choose a place without telephone or people interruptions.

5. Make sure all the lights are turned on. Lots of light always provides a positive atmosphere.

6. Turn off radios, beepers and other distractions.

Maintain Emotional Control

Assuming you have the right time and place, the next issue in assertive communication is not to lose your emotional control.

Maintaining control is at the heart of assertiveness. The person who asserts himself not only refuses to be manipulated by others, but also refuses to be controlled by his emotions.

We all need to recognize that attackers will usually target our feelings and emotions before they try to get to our thoughts. Emotions are easy prey for manipulation because they are so different from the functions of our rational thought processes. When we are functioning rationally, all aspects of the situation are considered.

When we function on emotion, most of our perspective is focused on one particular word or action. We can only see or hear one face, one accusing statement or one solution. Perspective is often missing when we have a knee-jerk response to confrontation.

Have you ever "lost it"? Most of us have. When we are "crazy in love" or "crazy with rage," we are outside the boundaries of reason.

If we admit there are times when our logic has nothing to do with how we feel, then the importance of maintaining control in a stressful confrontation becomes all the more important.

Let's face it, we all have buttons that can be pushed. There are words, gestures, phrases, subjects, personality traits and looks that trigger our "hot buttons."

When someone pushes the right buttons, we often say, "You made me angry." Is this true? No, because then you give someone permission to control your anger. An assertive person knows that anger is controlled from within. No one can *make* you angry. They can give you the incentive to be angry, but the decision for or against anger is up to you.

Easier said than done? Here are some strategies you can use the next time someone pushes all of your emotional hot buttons.

1. *Make a list of all your "buttons."* Familiarize yourself with these emotionally charged words, nonverbal gestures and subjects that trigger irrational feelings. Commit this list to memory. When you see or hear these items in a confrontation, you will maintain control. If you've decided this list will not control you, whatever is said will fail to provoke you.

2. *Practice self-talk.* If you know that a difficult encounter is coming up, role-play the conversation ahead of time. This practice session can help take the surprise out of your meeting.

3. *Concentrate on deep breathing.* Breathing is shallow and rapid when you are under extreme stress. You can maintain control of your mind and emotions if you keep your breathing deep and regular.

4. *Visualize the positive state of mind you will have when the confrontation is over.* Experience the relief and pride of

knowing you have assertively represented yourself. Take that satisfaction into the opening moments of your difficult meeting.

Here he comes! You decide not to be aggressive or passive. Today you will be assertive. You are not protecting yourself behind any ego defenses. It is the right time and place. You have control of your mind and emotions. What do you say first?

Begin with an "I" statement. An "I" statement represents what is going on inside you. This type of sentence is much different than the "you" statement, which gives responsibility and power to the other person.

To see the difference between the meaning of an "I" and "you" message, look at the two lists below.

"You" Messages

• "You really make me angry."

• "You messed up again."

• "You are the most disgusting person I know."

• "You hurt my feelings."

"I" Messages

• "I am angry about what you just said."

• "I think you were aware of these problems."

• "I feel frustrated because of these errors."

• "I think your behavior is unacceptable."

Read through the "you" statements again. Isn't there a definite feeling of defensiveness? Every time you begin a sentence with "you," you usually create a defensive attitude in your listener.

In addition to promoting defensiveness, "you" statements portray a basically nonassertive behavioral style. Whenever someone says, "You made me angry," he gives control and power to the other person. The admission that another person can make you angry is an admission of powerlessness (the position of the victim).

The "I" statement, on the other hand, is assertiveness at its best. Here is someone who is willing to take responsibility only for himself. There is no blaming or victimization.

Here he comes! It's OK. You, as the assertive communicator, have nothing to fear or protect. Your security, as you encounter this raging bull, is not in technique or tricks. You are comfortable with the possible confrontation because you are comfortable with yourself.

For Your Review

This chapter is about learning to confront as an assertive communicator. We learned that confrontation is not threatening to the assertive person because self-assertion does not fear being overwhelmed by someone else.

Review the information in this chapter by answering these questions:

1. When someone says, "I don't want to deal with that issue," is he using avoidance or repression?

2. Think back to a recent confrontation you had with someone you know well. Describe the setting, the time of day and your mood.

3. What is the best time of day to confront someone? Why?

4. Why should you choose a room without a telephone as a good place for a confrontation?

5. When someone pushes your "hot buttons," what will be your assertive response?

4

YOUR SILENT ASSERTIVE
COMMUNICATION

Have you ever screamed at someone without opening your mouth? Remember the look you sent across a room that would have pierced the hull of a battleship? Remember when you cleared your throat and brought the entire office to a sudden stop?

Sending a strong message without talking is a favorite communication game. We have discovered, since childhood, that sometimes our body language is louder than any words we can scream.

The assertive communicator has developed a much different set of nonverbal signals than either the aggressive or passive personality. Notice these differences in the comparative lists that follow.

Aggressive Body Language

Physical Appearance:

• Appears rigid.
• Hands placed on hips.
• Moves quickly from place to place.
• Walks ahead of others.
• Ready to lurch forward at any moment.

Facial Expressions:

• Lowers eyebrows.
• Rolls eyes upward to show displeasure.
• Mouth is turned down at corners.
• Turns head quickly for emphasis.

Gestures:

• Throws items.
• Slams doors.
• Jabs index finger into air at people.
• Uses a pencil or pen to direct people.
• Fingers are together when using the hand for emphasis.

Eye Contact:

• Stares.
• Moves quickly.
• Looks at clock or watch all the time.

Tone of Voice:

• Deliberate.
• Yells and screams for sustained periods of time.

Passive Body Language

Physical Appearance:

• Shoulders bent forward.

• Often leans on objects or walls.

• Slumps while sitting in chairs.

Facial Expressions:

• Blank.

• Eyes are looking down.

• Pouting.

• Inappropriate use of smiles.

Gestures:

• Constantly handling objects like coins, pens, paperclips, etc.

• Often chews on pens and pencils.

• Hands are at or over the mouth.

• Nodding of head in agreement.

Eye Contact:

• Does not make eye contact with other people.

• Looks to see how others are responding while someone is speaking to him.

• Excessive blinking.

Tone of Voice:

• Difficult to hear.

• Whiny.

• Fearful.

Assertive Body Language

Physical Appearance:

• At ease.

• Shoulders and back are straight.

• Open.

Facial Expressions:

• Interested.

• Reflects the appropriate tone of the conversation.

• Pleasant.

Gestures:

• When hands are used for emphasis, fingers are slightly apart.

• Arms and hands invite closeness.

• Index finger is directed to oneself.

Eye Contact:

• Periodically looks away.

• Makes direct eye contact.

Tone of Voice:

• Clear.

• Appropriate volume for the setting.

• Good modulation for emphasis.

Which personality type best describes you? Here are some interesting statistics about what we communicate face to face.

• 7% of what we communicate is words.

• 37% of what we communicate is tone of voice.

• 56% of what we transmit is facial expression and body language.

Knowing this should remind us that the real message is not in words but in our tone of voice and body language. And that our assertive messages are first communicated without ever saying a word.

Another important nonverbal message we send is through our appearance. What we are wearing, our makeup or lack of it, jewelry and a hundred other cues send strong messages about who we are and what the receiver can expect from us.

Appearance Guidelines for the Assertive Communicator

Clothes

It is best to invest in a few good clothes rather than have a full closet of less expensive items. Men should avoid blue jeans, cutoffs, t-shirts or other casual clothes inappropriate to the work environment. A basic two-button, single-breasted dark suit with white shirt and contrasting color tie always presents a positive image for a man.

Women should also choose a conservative approach. Simple lines, neutral-color dresses and pantsuits present a polished, professional image.

Jewelry

For both men and women, err on the side of simplicity. If a man wears as much jewelry around his neck and wrists as "Mr. T," you can be sure negative nonverbal messages will be bouncing all over the place.

Women should choose jewelry that is simple and use it sparingly. This jewelry should accent an outfit instead of being the outfit.

Hair

Hair, or the lack of it, does not communicate assertiveness. Men should wear hairstyles that communicate a comfortableness with aging — hairstyles that don't draw attention to a receding hairline.

Women should select a style appropriate to the shape of their face and body structure. But hairstyles should also be manageable. Spending hours in front of the mirror may not be the best use of your time.

Once someone starts to talk to you, what does your body language say about your willingness to listen? Experts have found we are effective listeners only 25 percent of the time. This means that three-quarters of our conversations are really one-way communication.

The assertive person works hard at projecting Unconditional Positive Regard (U.P.R.) when he listens. U.P.R. is a term that comes out of the therapy skills used by Dr. Carl Rogers. Dr. Rogers suggests that no one is willing to talk about the "real" issues unless the listener gives back unconditional positive regard. In other words, the speaker must be assured, nonverbally, that the listener sees the speaker as most important while the conversation is going on.

Unconditional Positive Regard

Unconditional positive regard is communicated by the listener in four ways:

1. The forward leaning position.

2. Eye contact.

3. Seating arrangement.

4. Parroting.

Forward Leaning Position

With one foot a few inches ahead of the other, you lean the upper part of your torso toward the speaker. This leaning into the other person is a nonverbal way of encouraging his thoughts. If you are seated, you should lean slightly forward in your chair. Make sure this isn't exaggerated. If the person senses you are about to fall over or invade his space, your leaning will have the opposite effect.

Eye Contact

When someone speaks to you, your eye contact is his first indication that you are interested. In our Western culture, it is appropriate to have intermittent eye contact.

Intermittent eye contact is characterized by moving your eyes from sustained contact (staring) to looking at other objects in your immediate environment. You can look briefly at the wall, floor, an earring, a tiebar, etc. without giving the other person a message that you really aren't listening.

But if you look repeatedly at other people in the same room, what is the nonverbal message? It can indicate a lack of interest. Looking at people and looking at a pair of draperies give two very different messages.

Also, don't continually look at your watch. Have you ever been talking to someone and while you were speaking, he tried to sneak a look at his wristwatch? How did you feel? The cursory look at a wristwatch is a signal screaming, "Sorry, pal, your time is up."

Assertive communication is enhanced with good eye contact marked by direct intermittent looks that say, "I'm listening."

Seating Arrangement

Large desks can become psychological demilitarized zones. How are your desk and chairs arranged in your office? What message(s) are you trying to give when a visitor walks into your space?

If you are leaning back in a high-backed executive chair looking at someone seated across your four-foot wide teakwood desk, what do you think this person hears from you even before you speak? The message is clear, "I hold the power here."

If you want to be a good listener, suggest that your visitor take a seat next to yours. As you sit with this person, instead of over this person, communication will be much easier.

Parroting

Here is a skill used effectively in psychotherapy.

Let's say someone comes into your office and says, "Since I have taken my new position, I have been so frustrated." You could say, "Now, sit down here and tell me what the problem is." But that response is much too general and isn't sensitive to the basic issue (frustration).

Follow the feelings here. After the person has said, "...I have been so frustrated," say, "Frustrated?" Notice this is an interrogatory statement. It is very important that you parrot or repeat back to the person the exact word he used, and put it in the form of a question.

Parroting gives the other person permission to discuss his feelings. Nine out of 10 times, the real issues have to do with feelings, not facts. You can argue all day about facts, but you can't argue with feelings. Feelings are just there.

Parroting can be overdone. Be careful not to overuse this tool or you will lose credibility.

For Your Review

Here are a few questions which may help to review what you have learned about nonverbal communication.

1. What are the silent messages I send when I am angry?

2. What percentage of my face-to-face communication is determined by my facial expressions?

3. In a business setting, what are the characteristics of assertive dress?

4. Unconditional positive regard is...

5. If someone said to me, "The position of my desk in our office makes me feel lonely," and I wanted to respond with parroting I would say...

5

RESOLVING CONFLICT
THROUGH ASSERTIVENESS

Conflict is good. However, most of us have been taught a far different message about conflict. As a child, do you remember what your parents said when they found you and a sibling arguing with each other? "You two stop that!" was probably what you heard.

"That" was conflict. We have been instructed, both verbally and nonverbally, that when two people disagree in thought or practice, it is best to just stay out of each other's way. We feel that conflict should be avoided because it only produces bad feelings and violent reactions.

It is true that some types of conflict are not good. History is punctuated with wars because conflicts became violent. Conflict can become irrational, and when the mind is unplugged, deadly results follow.

But conflict also has the potential to produce growth, adventure, opportunity and, ultimately, success. Conflict is good because it means two people care. If you don't care about a relationship there will be no energy to disagree or even fight. The opposite of love isn't hate — it's indifference.

Besides conflict being good, it is also unavoidable. Like sunrise tomorrow morning, conflict will always be with us. The issue is not how to eliminate conflict, but how to manage it effectively.

Assertive communication is the key to managing conflict. Regardless of the type of conflict — a neighbor who keeps dumping his grass clippings on your side of the fence, a child who insists on secretly borrowing your clothes, or a co-worker who habitually reads the mail on your desk — assertiveness is the only response that gives you the opportunity to resolve the conflict productively.

We do have other choices besides asserting ourselves in conflict. To clearly see the advantage of assertiveness, look at the five choices to conflict resolution as outlined by Lane Longfellow, a noted writer and lecturer.

Five Conflict Resolution Choices

1. Forcing

Here is a proven method of handling conflict. It is simple. Someone walks into a room, meets his adversary nose-to-nose and says loudly, "There is no problem here — we will just do it my way." Forcing imposes one person's will on another. In this method, there is no room for dialogue or debate. The conflict may be over for the moment, but not resolved.

2. Smoothing

Have you ever raised a question that created conflict but your opponent responded with, "There really isn't any conflict here because we both are saying the same thing." This attempt to gloss over the differences to create a pseudo-camaraderie is called smoothing. Usually a passive personality chooses this method.

3. Withdrawal

This method is the step beyond smoothing. After someone has tried to put a happy face on the conflict, he may say, "...hey, look at the time. I'm sorry but I have to pick up my laundry, and I just can't talk right now." This passive person is looking for an exit that will temporarily relieve the stress of dealing openly with conflict.

4. Compromise

Compromise depends on each person's willingness to give up something in order for both to win in a conflict. This method resolves conflict as long as each party feels the sacrifices are equal. If someone senses the final solution is weighted in one person's favor, the conflict will only bloom again. Compromise can be a quick solution, but often it is not permanent.

5. Confronting and Integrating

This is an assertive response to conflict. One person approaches the other and says, "We have a problem that I want to work on with you." There is no psychological game-playing or hidden agenda here. Someone begins the process by verbalizing what has been unsaid in passive-aggressive behavior. The process occurs when both parties express a desire to understand and then mesh their differing views. Integrating assumes respect for someone else's opinion and genuine caring that the relationship be repaired.

After looking at these five choices for resolving conflict, let's examine Confronting and Integrating, step-by-step, to see the specifics of an assertive response.

Confront and Integrate: An Assertive Conflict Response

1. *Define the conflict in terms of your needs.* Don't get caught in the "you" statement trap. While it may be easier to say, "You really make me sick with your list of demands," you gain more by saying, "I want to clearly communicate what my needs are." When you communicate your needs, you are

stating your position in the conflict. In effect, you are pouring the foundation on which the resolution can be built.

2. *Actively question the other person about possible solutions.* Don't do all the talking. Ask open-ended questions like, "Tell me what you think now that you know what my needs are," or, "Help me better understand your position." Once you have made a leading statement or asked a question, be quiet. Be patient, let silence stimulate an honest answer. (Remember, aggressive personalities answer for the other person.) Assertive people are self-confident enough to hear and accept the truth.

3. *Choose a solution that meets the needs of both parties.* Even if your agenda is complete, don't end the conversation unless the other person is satisfied as well. Conflict is not resolved if you have won and the other person has lost. If you question that, turn the equation around: Is the conflict over if your opponent won and you lost?

4. *Put together an action plan that gives both parties some responsibility.* If one person makes all the decisions and the solution doesn't resolve the conflict, guess who is responsible for the failure? If you and the other person are obligated to change, both of you are responsible for successfully resolving the conflict.

5. *Begin the action plan together.* At an agreed upon time, you and the other person should simultaneously implement the changes you discussed.

6. *Evaluate the solutions.* Your conflict resolution should include dates and times when the two of you will sit down and honestly ask, "How is this working?" If either of you is afraid to set those evaluation dates, there probably is a lack of confidence that the conflict will be resolved.

We have been talking about the assertive communicator's approach to conflict. Acting out that approach is the subject of the rest of this chapter. Let's begin to apply the approach with these eight principles of confronting conflict assertively.

Eight Principles of Assertively Confronting Conflict

Keep It Short

Have you ever been drawn into a conflict only to find that once you jumped in you couldn't find a way out? You just kept talking, hoping someone would rescue you? We often try to defend ourselves by using lots of words which become little shovels that dig us in deeper.

To keep yourself from becoming enmeshed in your own words, respond to conflict in short sentences such as, "I hear what you have said. It is my opinion that there are errors in your judgments of me. Here are the errors..."

Slow Down

Your first response to conflict is to reveal your feelings (often the faster the better). Your rate of speech will be a mile-a-minute. Unfortunately, when we speak rapidly, we often make mistakes or our mind races ahead of our ability to form the words.

Consciously discipline yourself to slow down when conflict begins. If you speak slowly, your thoughts sound much more logical.

Deepen Your Voice

Stress can tighten your vocal cords, making your voice sound higher than normal. This higher pitch sends a signal to your adversary that you are emotionally vulnerable.

If you feel your throat tighten, slow your speech. At the same time, make a determined effort to relax the muscles in your neck and shoulders. As you relax, you will hear a noticeable deepening of your voice.

Use a Firm Tone

What is the tone of your voice during conflict? To determine the possibilities of tone, repeat the following sentence as an aggressive, passive and assertive person: "I need a day off with pay."

Did you notice the firm quality of your assertive rendition? Notice the difference between a demanding, whining and firm tone when you listen to other people. Which do you react to positively?

Paraphrase

An effective tool of the assertive communicator is his ability to summarize what the other person has said. For instance, after listening to an angry co-worker comment on your habitual lateness with the monthly report, you may want to say, "So, you are saying my late reports make more work for you?"

You give your adversary two things when you paraphrase. First, you demonstrate that you've paid attention. Second, you offer "accurate empathy." Empathy is the quality of getting into someone else's shoes to feel what he feels.

Use Descriptions

Instead of making an accusatory generalization like, "You are always rude," you can clearly describe what has just happened by saying, "You just interrupted me."

Both of these statements begin with "you," but the second describes a fact. The first "you" statement is an opinion. It is easier to resolve a conflict when you are discussing facts.

Confirm the Facts

Give the other person the benefit of the doubt. If you are not sure exactly what someone is saying, ask. Instead of saying, "You hate my guts, don't you?" you may want to try, "Are you angry with me?"

Keep in Check

Some of our habitual behavior during conflict is self-preservation. Other reactions are bad habits we need to break. Following are some behaviors the assertive communicator will want to change:

• Don't interrupt someone's conversation.

• Don't answer for other people.

• Don't lose eye contact.

• Don't write notes while someone is speaking.

• Don't answer the phone during an emotional discussion.

• Don't act like a stone wall when someone asks for a response — give feedback.

• Don't label people or ideas.

• Don't play psychologist with, "I have figured out what your real problem is."

• Don't use loaded absolute terms such as "never" and "always."

Where do you experience conflict? In this final section, we will discuss settings where most of us will be in the center of conflict. As you become an assertive communicator, you can use your new skills in these scenarios.

Common Conflict Settings

1. Telephone Interruptions

You have a deadline to submit a proposal at 5 p.m. today. The telephone rings. You don't want to answer it, but there is a possibility the caller may be your boss. Against your better judgment you pick up the receiver. Your worst fear is realized — it's your mother.

You have several options: You could pretend there is static on the line and say it is difficult to hear her. You could keep working while saying an occasional "un-huh" to let her think you are listening. You could scream something about your life passing in front of you if you don't get this proposal finished. Or you could say, "I cannot talk right now because I have a 5 p.m. deadline. I will call you later tonight."

Instead of responding to the manipulation of authority ("What's the matter, too high and mighty to take five minutes to talk to your own mother?") or the guilt ("No really, it's O.K. I'll call you the next time from the hospital."), you choose to honestly assert yourself.

If your telephone is becoming more of a liability than an asset you might want to try:

- Having someone screen your calls.

- Using short "I" messages.

- Arranging a time to have someone call you back.

- Taking the phone off the hook.

2. *Out-of-the-Blue Visitors*

If people are popping in from nowhere you can:

a. Have someone screen your visitors.

b. Stand up as soon as someone comes into your work area. If you remain seated, the other person physically is in charge of the amount of time he will spend.

c. Say, "I know this issue is important to you, but I only have five minutes to spend with you."

d. Ask: "How much time do you think this issue will take?" This allows your visitor to set the time limits, which you can amend or enforce later with, "...as I mentioned earlier, I have another appointment in just a minute."

3. *Drop-the-Ball Workers*

Have you ever said, "If you want to get anything done right, you have to do it yourself"? Has your answer kept you working until 8 p.m. or all weekend? Delegation is the skill of accomplishing your goals through others. Sometimes other people don't cooperate.

If conflict arises when your employee resists delegation, try some of these assertive responses:

- "Yes, you may feel overworked, but this task must be done by Tuesday."

- "This job seems difficult for you. Why?"

- "This job still is not finished. I feel angry and frustrated because I gave you the tools and time to get it done. When can I expect the task to be completed?"

An assertive adult does not have to apologize for expressing what he wants. If you are the employer, you should expect accountability in response to your requests.

4. Yup-Hound Syndrome

Yup hounds are people who say "yup" or yes to almost any request. These overly agreeable people are part of this chapter on conflict resolution because if you are the Yup Hound, you probably are up to your ears in bad feelings for yourself.

An inability to say "no" to others' subtle or overt demands comes out of a false sense of obligation. Obligation was instilled in us as children with a list of "shoulds." You should be quiet in church; you should be good; you should brush your teeth after every meal; etc.

Because of the "shoulds," you may be unable to say "no." But if you can't say "no," you create more demands on your time and energy.

Here are five steps you can take when you decide to give an assertive "no."

1. Listen to the other person attentively.

2. Say "no" at the beginning of the conversation so you don't build false hope.

3. Give specific reasons why you are saying "no."

4. Offer alternatives so the other person will have some positive options in the wake of your refusal.

5. Thank the person for asking.

When we cannot say "no," we often internalize the anger that results from taking on more than we can get done. We are not angry with the person who made the request — we are angry with ourselves for not establishing appropriate limits. This is a passive response.

An assertive person is always left with good feelings, not about refusing, but about being honest.

For Your Review

This chapter discussed the assertive communicator's approach to conflict. We learned that assertive skills are especially useful because conflict is not a power-play but a set of decisions about finding solutions.

To integrate these ideas, answer these questions or situations.

1. Give a reason, as an assertive communicator, why the statement "Conflict is good" is true.

2. Of the five options to conflict (Forcing, Smoothing, Withdrawal, Compromise, Confronting and Integrating), which would the assertive communicator choose? Why?

3. How do you consciously lower your voice when you are involved in verbal conflict?

4. You have been talking to someone on the telephone for the last 15 minutes. You have to keep an appointment in five minutes. How do you assertively conclude the conversation?

5. Someone is taking advantage of you. You have not said "no" to this person in the last year. Now he is making another unreasonable request. How do you assertively say "no"?

6

ASSERTIVE COMMUNICATION WITH SUPERVISORS

Let's face it, supervisors have something we don't — power. You may be intimidated by a supervisor because he wields power. Behind the titles on mahogany doors or engraved nameplates on large desks is the subtle reminder that supervisors are the architects of our future.

Like striking a match, power has the potential to destroy or create. Supervisors who use their power thoughtfully can empower workers to professional success and personal growth. Ninety percent of all supervisors use their positions to enable people to achieve personal goals.

The assertive communicator is not threatened by a supervisor's power. Assertiveness enhances one's own authority because thoughts and feelings are accurately represented.

An assertive worker can fulfill his job description and, at the same time, not deny his feelings or thoughts as long as they are expressed at the appropriate time and place, and in an appropriate manner. If assertiveness is seen as a force for positive change by both the worker and the supervisor, there is no threat to either person.

Assuming assertiveness is a positive force in your relationship with your supervisor, closely examine these eight needs of all supervisors. Especially note the suggested responses of the assertive communicator.

Eight Needs of a Supervisor

1. Supervisors need a challenge.

Supervisors are motivated by the challenge of the task. As a matter of fact, when the task becomes more difficult, these people are more turned on.

The aphorism you may hear in your supervisor's office is, "We don't have a problem here — we just have a decision." After all, satisfying a customer in Detroit or getting a product to London before next Wednesday are the challenges this person has successfully met to get to his present position.

The assertive communicator needs to remember that when people get in the way of accomplishing the task, the supervisor feels challenged. When you frustrate the efficient plans of your supervisor, the challenge has been made. Now you are the problem your supervisor is challenged to solve.

The assertive communicator has to accomplish two goals in a confrontation with a supervisor. First, the supervisor must feel he still has control. Second, you must retain your self-confidence.

Here is an example of an assertive employee, Susan, in conversation with her supervisor, Lois.

Lois: "Susan, these mailing lists need to be updated immediately and sent down to Receiving by 5 p.m."

Susan: "It is impossible for me to update those lists and also finish the report you requested yesterday. Which project is the priority?"

Lois: "I need the mailing lists done first."

Notice that Susan could have challenged Lois. A response like, "There is no way I can update the mailing lists along with everything else I have to do," would only have challenged Lois to be more demanding. For Lois, updating the mailing list was the priority. If Susan had not been assertive, she would have become the focus of the problem by not finishing either task on time or by choosing the wrong one to complete first.

2. Supervisors need everyone to play by the same rules.

No one likes the rules changed in the middle of the game. Supervisors feel frustrated when workers try to rearrange their rules.

Changing the rules is only acceptable when the initiative comes from the supervisor. Assertiveness can encourage changes, but it is critical that the supervisor feel the change was his idea, initiated on his timetable.

Notice the interaction between Chuck and his supervisor, Jennie. Yesterday at coffee break, a conversation centered around the need for men to wear neckties to work during the summer months. Chuck was very vocal in his support for dropping this dress requirement. There was some natural humor expressed by both Chuck and Jennie on the necktie issue as everyone went back to their work stations. Later that afternoon, Chuck asks for a few minutes of Jennie's time in her office.

Chuck: "I know we laughed about neckties at break this morning, but I would like to make a serious suggestion. Why not give the men the option to not wear neckties and allow women to wear slacks on Fridays during the summer."

Jennie: "Is this your idea or are you speaking for others?"

Chuck: "I'm speaking just for myself, and I have not talked with anyone else about this."

Jennie: "Give me some time to think about it."

Chuck had several other choices. First, he could have come to work without a necktie and forced a "show-down" with Jennie using passive-aggressive behavior. Second, Chuck could have lobbied others in the office to produce a "gang" atmosphere for his demand. Third, Chuck could have ripped off his tie during coffee break and said, "In this weather, wearing ties is probably the most asinine rule this company ever dreamed up."

All of these responses would have directly challenged the rules and the authority of those who made them. Jennie and all supervisors would have become defensive when the rules were broken or changed without their consent.

3. Supervisors work by the clock.

Supervisors insist on keeping a specific schedule and demand others use their time efficiently.

Tom is Isaac's supervisor. They have always had a precise business relationship. Isaac recognizes Tom's need for specific time parameters. Notice how Isaac anticipates this need.

Tom: "These product reports will have to be revised for next Wednesday's staff meeting."

Isaac: "How much time do you think that will take me?"

Tom: "Two hours max."

Isaac: "As I look over them, I need at least three. Here are the reasons I will need three hours to complete the revisions... What do you think?"

Isaac asked up front about Tom's expectations of the time the task would require. The assertive communicator allows the supervisor to set the limits and then gives specific reasons why those limits are either achievable or unrealistic. The most important point of this encounter was Isaac's assertive role in making the supervisor design the timeframe. Isaac's honest response allows both people to assert their needs without resorting to manipulation or power plays.

4. Supervisors need concise conversations.

Supervisors don't want to chat. They know how to shoot the breeze, but when it comes to work there is no time for chatting.

When you take a long time to explain something to your supervisor, watch for the nonverbal signals of impatience. There will be shifting of weight from one foot to the other, loss of eye contact, occasional glances at a watch or clock and erratic hand movements.

The assertive communicator knows business conversations need to be succinct. You may want to make a few notes on a 3 x 5 index card before walking into your supervisor's office. Your ability to be concise will be appreciated.

Rita approaches her supervisor, Carol, with a request for a day off. Carol is intently working on paperwork at her desk.

Rita: "Carol, can I talk with you for three minutes?"

Carol: "Come on in, Rita, what can I do for you?"

Rita: "I would like to take the day off next Friday. Here are the reasons I am making this request. First, I need to take my son to the orthodontist for his final visit. And, second, I'm feeling some emotional exhaustion right now, and I think the day off would make me more effective when I get back to work on Monday."

Notice Rita did not initiate the conversation by asking, "...talk with you for just three minutes." Rita is planning on three minutes or less and did not need "just" to justify her request. Also, Rita has given Carol the reasons for the request using numerical conjunctions, "first" and "second." Carol, as a supervisor, works best when she can delineate information in specific categories.

5. Supervisors need results.

When all is said and done, it is the bottom line that ultimately catches your supervisor's attention.

Assertive communication with a supervisor should ultimately center in on the final product. Meeting this need has profound implications on how you structure your conversations. Begin by letting your supervisor know how your conversation will produce a new or better product.

Jane has decided to make an appointment to talk with her supervisor, Dave, about a change in the layout of the company brochure. This publication will be printed in five days. Jane begins the conversation by saying, "I am making suggestions on the new brochure that will increase sales by 10 percent over the next six months and eliminate the cost of hiring another staff person in the mailroom."

Using this approach, Jane will get Dave's attention. Phrases like, "increase our sales by 10 percent" and "eliminate the cost" are bottom-line items for the supervisor. Jane did not introduce those specific items by saying, "If I could, I would like to make suggestions." There is no permission-seeking in Jane's approach to Dave. Jane will honestly identify with Dave's need to deal with bottom-line items without apology.

6. *Supervisors need you to be aware of their authority.*

This doesn't mean supervisors want you to kneel to their every word. It means that when there is a choice between your authority and their authority, you will always choose theirs.

Assertiveness is honest and smart. You can state what your needs are, but always conclude with a request that the supervisor determine how the situation be handled if it comes up again.

Sam is offended because Joan, his supervisor, has just pulled Nathan, a member of Sam's staff, off a project that Sam had assigned. Sam makes an appointment to talk with Joan.

Sam: "I need your help with a staff issue."

Joan: "What's the problem?"

Sam: "I'm confused. Nathan had an assignment from me to finish the Clark file. Nathan told me an hour ago that you moved him to another job for the rest of the afternoon. I know you must really be under the gun to do something like that without asking me first. I'm sure you will agree that if that practice continues, it will create confusion around here."

Joan: "I just couldn't think of anyone else who was free right now."

Sam: "I understand your problem, but now I have a problem too. Pulling my people off jobs I have assigned without my consent is unacceptable to me. Please help me come up with a plan to make sure you have emergency help in the future, and I can get my assignments done as well."

Sam was not aggressive — he was assertive. Without threatening the authority of Joan, Sam stated what his needs were and then turned control of any future situations over to Joan.

7. Supervisors need workers to take the initiative.

The average supervisor in the United States spends three to four hours a day on routine paper work. Most of a supervisor's day is filled with the tyranny of putting out fires or "getting monkeys off his back." These people do not have a lot of time for creativity.

The assertive communicator is especially attractive to the supervisor because he enjoys managing a worker who can take the initiative without requiring more managerial time.

Ken notices that Bud has been running from one meeting to the next during the last few days. Ken also knows that Bud's annual supervision report has to be finished by the end of this week. Ken pulls Bud aside and says, "I know you are burning the candle at both ends to get the annual report finished. My part of the report will be on your desk tomorrow, and I have reminded everyone else on staff to have their reports to you."

Ken didn't have to remind the rest of the staff. Assertiveness is an attitude that enables others, including supervisors, to achieve their goals.

8. Supervisors don't like surprises.

The best way to communicate with a supervisor is in writing. Clear, short memos usually warm the cockles of any supervisor's overworked heart.

As the assertive worker takes the initiative, works through the process, and produces a better product, the supervisor should be kept informed. Here is a good piece of assertive communication.

> "Harry, at this Wednesday's strategy meeting, you should expect the following:
>
> 1. Sandy will highlight the areas of the country where our sales are up.
>
> 2. I will present a request for a 40 percent increase in our advertising budget.
>
> 3. I have definite information that our competitor has a copy of last year's sales figures.
>
> I know some of this isn't the best news, but I wanted to give you time to consider your response."

After looking at your supervisor's needs and the assertive responses, you may be saying to yourself, "I still haven't heard the normal encounter I have with my supervisor." In the next section, you may find you and your supervisor as we look at typical situations where the employee needs to assert himself.

Situations That Call for an Assertive Response

"This Isn't My Job"

If a supervisor approaches you with a new responsibility that is not part of your job description, you can be:

Aggressive: "Sorry, that isn't my job, and there is no way you can make me do it."

Passive: "I will get it done ASAP."

Assertive: "I am confused by your request. I don't see this task in my job description. Are you expanding my job responsibilities? If you are, I will have to delay some of my regular duties."

The assertive person has not rewritten the rules. If there is a new assignment, it will mean another required responsibility will have to be delayed.

"This Is Wrong"

You are out in the middle of the work area. There are co-workers close to your desk who can easily overhear your conversation with your supervisor.

Walking confidently up to your desk, your supervisor says, "These figures from last month's report are incorrect." Your choices are:

Aggressive: "You are wrong. I checked them three times, and I know they are right."

Passive: "If you think so — they must be wrong."

Assertive: "What evidence do you have that they are wrong?"

The question requesting evidence will make your supervisor deal with the bottom line. You are not challenging, you are merely asking for factual proof that will substantiate his position. If you are wrong, don't apologize. The assertive communicator will say, "You are right, I was wrong. These will be corrected immediately."

"About My Annual Performance Review..."

You have just received a copy of your supervisor's comments on your annual performance review. In your opinion, your supervisor has unjustly evaluated your abilities. How do you respond?

Aggressive: "I have a bone to pick with you. What were you smoking the day you wrote my annual performance review?"

Passive: (will not confront)

Assertive: "I found some inconsistencies with your comments on my annual performance review and what you have said both verbally and in written correspondence."

Since your supervisor likes brevity and the bottom line, you will have to produce either copies of memos or dates of conversations when he gave another message to you about your performance. If there are areas where criticism is justified, you may want to say, "I need some suggestions on how to improve in these areas." This will reaffirm the supervisor's authority.

"I Deserve a Raise"

You believe you deserve a raise. You have arranged a private appointment to discuss a salary increase with your supervisor. Here are some of your options:

Aggressive: "You have tried to keep me under your thumb for years by paying me dirt. I won't stand for it any longer. Either you give me a 50 percent raise, or I'm history around here."

Passive: "You are not going to like this — but...but I would like you to think about...if you could...and there isn't any pressure here...a small raise."

Assertive: "After reviewing the company policy manual and honestly appraising my skills, I deserve a raise for these specific reasons... I want your response to this request."

There is no apology in the assertive response. Here is someone who has factual information on why a raise is merited. Supervisors respond well to this type of presentation.

What if your supervisor doesn't respond well to this or any of the other assertive responses that have been suggested in this chapter? What if your supervisor responds with anger and hostility? Let's be honest — assertiveness, regardless of the assertive communicator's expertise, is threatening to some supervisors.

If you receive a defensive response from your supervisor, keep these principles in mind:

1. *Don't push.* Assertiveness is for you; you cannot make others communicate honestly and assertively. Forcing others to view the world through your eyes is taking responsibility for someone else.

2. *Avoid public debates on assertiveness with your supervisor.* Your supervisor may decide the only way to maintain control is to publicly entice you into an argument. Keep emotional and mental control of yourself when your buttons are pushed. Stick to discussing the facts objectively.

3. *Speak only for yourself.* A natural protective response to an aggressive supervisor might be, "Well, I'm not the only one around here who feels this way..." There is no protection in that statement. As a matter of fact, not only will the supervisor become more defensive, he will see the inherent manipulation in that weak tactic.

4. *Maintain your assertive skills.* You are not responsible for satisfying your supervisor's threatened ego. Assertiveness satisfies your need to look in the mirror and like the person you see. If you lose yourself for eight hours, it may be difficult to find the real you the other 16.

5. *Get Help.* If your supervisor becomes verbally, emotionally or physically abusive in response to your assertive behavior, find someone who will hear your grievance and take disciplinary action to make sure this victimization does not continue.

For Your Review

In this chapter, we learned your supervisor has some specific needs which can be met without giving up your assertive rights. We reviewed specific assertive responses to the needs of: challenge, playing by the rules, punctuality, concise conversations, bottom-line results, maintaining authority, taking the initiative and staying informed.

More than just meeting these needs, we discovered you can actually empower your supervisor and yourself, through assertiveness, to achieve your mutual goals.

As a result of reading this chapter, you may want to write down specific assertive responses to these scenarios as you communicate with your supervisor:

1. You are requesting a raise.

2. You have been unjustly evaluated in an annual performance review.

3. You have been passed over for a promotion.

4. You received an assignment which is not part of your job description.

5. You have factual proof that your supervisor lied to you.

7

ASSERTIVE COMMUNICATION
WITH PEERS AND EMPLOYEES

Let's turn the tables. In Chapter 6 we learned some specific assertive communication skills with the power-brokers in our lives, our supervisors. In this chapter we will again examine power: the power of self-confidence as you assertively communicate with your peers and employees.

Peers and employees are two very different groups of people. Peers are those people who work *with* you. Employees are those people who work *for* you.

With peers, there are no strings attached. They do not write your annual review or sign your payroll check, but they are, nevertheless, very important. Peers provide a positive social atmosphere that can make work rewarding.

Employees are important too because through them we accomplish our professional goals. If you are a manager, your product will never be produced unless you rely on others.

Both of these groups require different and specific assertive communication skills. Notice these skills depend on the assertive communicator's self-confidence and his inner strength, not his ability to intimidate.

Assertive Communication With Peers

We normally assume that peers will be brutally honest in their communication with us. After all, these people can say what they want without concern for their professional future. But is this true?

Even though honesty should be the hallmark of communication between peers, word-games and nonverbal messages often become ingrained behavior between people on the same vocational level. Why? To preserve an important relationship we may find covert ways to say the things we cannot put into words. Often a peer will say one thing and mean another. For example:

What is Said	*What is Meant*
"I was just being honest."	"You cannot handle hearing the truth."
"Naturally, you will want to come."	"I am expecting you to be there."
"Are you still here?"	"You should have been gone by this time."
"I was merely making a point."	"You are not reasonable."
"You certainly are quiet."	"Your silence is driving me crazy because I don't know what you are thinking."
"Come on, let's relax."	"You are tense, and I don't like being with you."
"You tried your best, I'm sure."	"You did not try hard enough."

Notice the purpose of each comment is to say something covertly which the person is afraid to say openly. Since the intent is to hide the real meaning, an assertive response should identify the real issue and ask for clarification. *Here are two steps to take when you hear a covert message from a peer:*

1. Repeat the message in your mind, rehearsing the rhythm and pitch of the speaker's voice.

2. Say out loud what you think the real message is, and ask the other person if you have interpreted this message accurately.

Let's apply these two assertive skills with the assertive responses on the right.

Covert Message	*Assertive Response*
"You sure have been tired lately."	"You sound bothered that I have been tired. Has my tiredness inconvenienced you?"
"I was just being honest."	"That statement implies I'm not able to accept an honest evaluation. I would like to hear your honest and objective opinion of the situation."
"Naturally, you will want to come."	"You are expecting me to be there. How will you feel if I do not show up?"
"Are you still here?"	"Does it bother you that I'm working late? Why?"
"I was merely making a point."	"That statement says to me you think I am unreasonable. Is that true?"
"You certainly are quiet."	"Does my silence bother you? Why?"

"Come on, let's relax."	"You must see me as being uptight right now. Is that true?"
"You tried your best, I'm sure."	"You obviously don't think I tried hard enough. Be specific about what else I should have done."
"Now, what do you want?"	"You seem irritated. Do you think I complain a lot?"

These specific assertive responses cut through to the real message and make it possible for you to communicate without covert attacks.

Assertive Communication With Employees

Management means accomplishing your goals through other people. As long as other people cooperate, management is a breeze. When employees do not cooperate, management can seem impossible.

Employees know all of this. The people who work for you understand that their willingness to adopt your goal is the secret to success. Employees can frustrate management when they decide to resist management's goals.

You need specific assertive skills to communicate with your employees. The following five difficult personalities illustrate effective assertive responses.

The Whiner

This person has lost power. Here is the eternal victim. Everyone and everything victimizes this person. The Whiner suffers from what Dr. Martin E. P. Seligman, a noted psychologist from the University of Pennsylvania, calls "learned helplessness." Dr. Seligman says people with the helplessness syndrome have been taught how to be helpless.

The syndrome starts when someone offers to do everything for the Whiner. As long as the helping continues, so does the helplessness. In other words, when we indulge people with vast amounts of social or emotional care, there is no need for them to help themselves — we create helplessness.

The Whiner complains constantly. By becoming obnoxious (the whining voice quality), the Whiner indulges in the only power available to him — the ability to get attention.

The assertive communicator uses these skills to deal with a Whiner:

1. Keep a diary of the dates, times and places a Whiner complains.

2. Record your feelings in the diary whenever you are exposed to the Whiner.

3. Commit the facts in the diary to memory.

4. Wait until the Whiner complains again and then ask to meet this person privately.

5. From memory, give the Whiner the specific dates, times and places he complained.

6. Use this expression, "I am frustrated because I do not enjoy being around you when you are complaining. As I have pointed out, complaining is a major part of our working relationship. I am willing to help you solve specific problems. Let's define them and discuss possible solutions."

This list addresses two important issues with the Whiner. First, you are confronting. The Whiner normally takes the initiative to gain power in the conversation. You have short-circuited that habitual behavior.

Second, your verbal response makes the Whiner part of the solution. In focusing on solutions, you have broken the learned helplessness syndrome.

The Time Bomb

Do you know someone who walks around ready to explode? The wrong look, comment or setting can ignite an inappropriate venting of anger. This person seems to be looking for a fight.

Notice the manipulation in the Time Bomb's behavior. Time Bombs prevent us from expressing our thoughts and emotions because we don't want to trigger the next "scene." Also, Time Bombs usually never explode in one-on-one circumstances.

These people need a crowd because they know most people won't fight back in front of a group. Time Bombs are unpredictable at best; who knows what this person will do if someone starts to scream back?

Here are assertive actions to take with a Time Bomb the next time he explodes near you:

1. Let the person vent his inappropriate behavior (use of four-letter words, flailing of arms, screaming, etc.). If you begin yelling or using some of the same inappropriate techniques, the Time Bomb will have accomplished one of his goals — to gain power by making you lose control. Wait until the tirade is over before you say anything to this person.

2. Immediately after the scene, ask this person to meet you in a private place.

3. When the door is closed you may want to begin with this statement, "I am furious. What happened a few minutes ago in this office is unacceptable to me. You have a right to be angry, but you do not have a right to attack me and others. I want to know what we can do to make sure this scene never happens again."

4. If the Time Bomb doesn't think there is anything inappropriate about his display of anger, you need to continue to make "I" statements that represent how you feel.

5. You may want to arrange a "behavioral contract" with this person. This contract gives you permission to intervene when the Time Bomb explodes. The Time Bomb may genuinely want to break these old behavioral patterns, but needs help from you to identify what sets him off.

The Fox

The Fox has the unique ability to walk up to you with an ear-to-ear smile, make a few humorous comments, leave you smiling and before you realize it you have been mortally wounded.

You may hear, "Hey, you look great today. I really like that outfit. That blouse looks especially good with your hair color. How would you describe your hair color this week?" Everyone has a good laugh — at your expense.

The Fox has perfected verbal skills that allow him to zing you when you least expect it. Again, using a crowd to control your response, this person uses fear and guilt to manipulate. You fear the response you get if you respond, and the guilt is, "How can I attack a fun-loving person?"

Behind the smiling exterior is a frightened person. The Fox is usually insecure and intent on keeping everyone at arm's length with a philosophy of, "People will have you for lunch if you get too close."

An assertive communicator may want to use this strategy:

1. Never take this person on in a group. If he is a true Fox, he will overpower you. His skill with words and humor make him a formidable foe.

2. Ask the Fox to meet you alone.

3. Here is an opening assertive statement, "I am angry because your humor embarrassed me." Follow this with specific feelings. Relate your feelings to particular comments he made.

4. You may want to add, "I don't think the color of my hair (or the soup stains on my tie) are the real issues between the two of us. What is the real issue here?"

5. What have you gained with this private confrontation? You have assertively told the Fox that you refuse to be the passive butt of his humor in the future.

The Stone Wall

You confront someone and he gives you zip, zero, zilch in return. There is nothing — no words, no eye contact, no body language. This person is nothing more than a stone wall.

Probably the Stone Wall learned this behavior as a child. Initially, stone-walling may have been a reaction to an unexpected crisis; the pain of that moment was so excruciating that this person was not able to give any response. But by not responding, he may have learned that other people will leave him alone. Then stone-walling becomes learned behavior with the intent of keeping people away.

Assuming that the Stone Wall is manipulating you with this non-responsive behavior, you can confront him this way:

1. Ask the Stone Wall to meet you somewhere private.

2. Begin with, "I'm sure you are feeling upset right now, and you probably don't want to talk. I do. I am frustrated because you and I have to work together and communicate. Right now, the communication is one-way and we both know that will never work. As difficult as it may be, I need to hear what you are thinking and feeling. I may not like what I hear, but I am ready to deal with whatever you have to say."

3. Give the person time to respond. Don't try to fill the silence with words.

4. After a certain period of time, if there has been no response, say, "I know this is difficult for you, but I must know what you are thinking and feeling in order for us to work together."

5. If there is still no response, you might want to say, "This issue is not over for me. Tomorrow morning at 9 a.m. I will ask you the same question again. I hope you will feel more comfortable discussing this with me then."

It is important that you do not allow the Stone Wall to go unchallenged. Every time you tolerate the stone-walling behavior, you only encourage the same response in the future.

The Procrastinator

Maybe you have met this difficult person — in the mirror.

We all know what it is like to put off until tomorrow what we should have done today. Most of us don't know why we keep procrastinating.

Dr. Wayne Dyer, in his best-selling book, *Your Erroneous Zones*, says procrastinators are people who fear the pain of being wrong. Behind that definition is a need for perfectionism.

Perfection is an illusion. Perfectionism doesn't exist. There is always some flaw that drifts across the landscape of our best efforts.

People who are perfectionists have an over-developed conscience, and guilt is their constant partner. There is never enough data to write the perfect report. There are never enough sales for the end-of-the-month reports. There are never enough erasers in the stockroom.

If you know people who nitpick their way through life trying desperately to produce the perfect product, you may want to use this assertive plan:

1. When reports or projects are late, arrange a personal conversation with the Procrastinator.

2. Begin, "I know you want this report to be complete. So do I. But right now the report is two weeks late. What steps are you going to take to get the report done?"

3. In that statement you have empathized with his need for perfectionism, but have reminded the Procrastinator of the realities of life.

4. You may also want to help the Procrastinator break the project or task into small manageable pieces.

5. By far, the best assertive response to a Procrastinator is to remind him he still has worth.

The loss of worth or value ("I am wrong") is what keeps this person immobilized and unable to make decisions.

For Your Review

Peers are people linked to us because we often occupy the same work space. These people give us acceptance and affirmation about both our job performance and our shared humanity.

Assertive communication skills are especially important when receiving dual messages from our peers — when someone says one thing and means another. The assertive person learns to evaluate and clarify the unstated message.

Employees understand they are essential to accomplishing our goals at work. When you are frustrated by a difficult employee, you should confront not only the behavior, but your employee's intent.

In reviewing this chapter, decide how you would respond assertively to these situations:

1. A peer walks up to your desk on Monday morning and says, "My, aren't we dressed fit to kill today."

2. In a staff meeting, a peer says in front of your boss, "You don't really believe management will buy that?"

3. You have just walked into the office after one of your employees screamed obscenities at another worker.

4. You have asked an employee, for the fourth time, when a sales report will be finished. The employee looks at you but says nothing.

5. For the sixth time this week, an employee comes into your office to complain.

8

ASSERTIVE COMMUNICATION
WITH CUSTOMERS

"The customer is always right." Do you believe that? If you do, you need to become an assertive communicator.

Are you ever right in a dispute with a customer? Are there times when the customer is wrong?

These are important questions because they expose the fallacy in American business of making the customer the arbitrator of all truth. If the customer is *always* right, it follows that those who make or sell the product are *always* wrong. That is an inaccurate, passive assumption.

An assertive communicator assumes, as in all human relationships, that some of the time one or both parties will be wrong and that often both parties share responsibility for a problem. With that balanced view, let's look at five situations where you and your customer will be best served through assertive skills.

The For-Profit Customer

If you sell someone a washing machine, automobile or new house, the product has to meet the customer's needs. When your customer's shirts come out of the washer shredded, his car continually needs repair or the roof on his new house leaks, be prepared for complaints.

In a for-profit sale, the lines of accountability are clear. The product must fulfill the promises made, or the customer will seek compensation.

Before we look at a specific assertive strategy for handling a customer's complaints, there are two essential rules to know about all complaints:

> 1. The 6-10 rule.
>
> 2. The 3-11 rule.

The 6-10 Rule states: "For every 10 people who say they are going to complain, six of them will never show up."

The 3-11 Rule states: "Every satisfied customer will tell three other people about your product or service. Every dissatisfied customer will tell 11 other people."

These two rules highlight how important it is to handle a customer's complaint quickly and with sensitivity. In every complaint there are two factors:

1. Fact —   Specifically what went wrong with the product or service.

2. Feeling — How the customer feels about the failure of the product or service.

Both of these issues must be addressed when responding to the complaint.

An Assertive Strategy for Handling Customer Complaints

Here is an assertive strategy to use when listening to a customer's complaint.

1. Listen attentively. Let the customer get his feelings off his chest. You may want to help the person focus on the facts with a question like, "What exactly went wrong with the product?" As you listen, use the skills of paraphrasing, parroting and intermittent eye contact. These skills will let the person know you genuinely care about the facts and his feelings.

2. Offer an explanation. If there was a labor strike that delayed delivery, a defective part from another supplier, or you made a mistake — admit it openly. The assertive person has nothing to fear in saying, "I am at fault because I did not send in your order on time."

3. Offer alternatives. If you can replace the defective item, do it. The customer may not always be right, but the customer should always be satisfied. You may offer to replace the defective product or return the customer's money. It is best to give the customer several options to choose from so he participates in solving the problem.

4. Thank the customer. Complaints are good. You will not know what to fix in the future if you don't know what is wrong in the present. Remember, when 10 customers are not satisfied, only four of them will tell you. If you develop a reputation for listening to complaints, customers will complain to *you*, not potential customers.

What if you have done your best to respond to a customer's complaints but he is still not satisfied?

An appropriate assertive response might be, "I have suggested all the possible solutions to solve your problem. I will work hard to make sure you are pleased with the final solution, but there are certain things I cannot do. Let me repeat what I can and cannot do... Do you have any further suggestions?"

This response gives your customer the boundaries in which you are able to help him.

Not-for-Profit Customers

If you work for a government agency, charity, religious group, community service agency or any other not-for-profit organization, you face unique challenges with "customers."

In a for-profit transaction, money establishes lines of accountability. If you hire someone to paint your house and he only does half the job, you can reduce the amount you pay. When you are involved in a not-for-profit environment, accountability is blurred by issues such as power and influence. To illustrate this point, let's look at the interaction between Donna, a staff member at a community service organization, and one of the organization's board members who is the head of a large company in the community.

Donna: "Mr. Jackson, I need to discuss the solicitation letters with you."

Mr. Jackson: "Well, Donna let's do it another time. I've got some calls I need to make."

Donna: "I need only five minutes of your time. This fundraising program is of critical importance."

Mr. Jackson: "All right. What can I do for you?"

Donna: "As you recall, each board member agreed to write six personal letters to members of the business community asking them to support our Fall fund drive. The board established a deadline of October 15 for the letters to be completed. We have not received your letters. Is there a problem?"

Mr. Jackson: "I have been very busy."

Donna: "I can appreciate the demands on your time. I also appreciate your commitment to our organization and the contributions you have made. And these letters are a very important part of your contribution. How can I help you get them done?"

Mr. Jackson: "Well, I'm leaving town next Tuesday for three weeks, and I just won't have time to draft those letters before I leave."

Donna: "Let me make a suggestion. I will prepare a draft of the letter and have it for you tomorrow. Can you give me 20 minutes of your time to review the letters? Then I can have them prepared and you can sign them on Monday before you leave."

Mr. Jackson: "That will be fine."

Donna did not allow herself to be intimidated by Mr. Jackson's position of power and his resistance to writing the letters. She reminded him of his obligation and the deadline, practiced reflective listening by indicating she knew he was busy, continued to assert her need for the letters, and then negotiated an acceptable solution.

In this type of situation, Donna has no power or authority that she can use to make Mr. Jackson honor his commitment. Using emotionally-charged pressure tactics like guilt would only create problems. Instead, Donna asserted herself by staying focused on the objective and seeking a practical, workable solution to the problem.

Front-Line Customers

If you sit in an office or reception area continually encountering customers you have never met before, you deal with Front-Line Customers.

Front-Line Customers are unique in three ways. First, you have no history with these people. Second, the response these people want is usually immediate. Third, there may be no opportunity to follow up with these customers to see if their needs have been satisfied.

Taking these unique circumstances into account, here are some typical encounters an assertive communicator may have with these customers.

Customer: "I want to speak to your boss right now!"

Response: "May I have your name, please."

Customer: "You don't need my name, but I need your boss!"

Response: "I cannot call my supervisor unless I know your name and the reason for your visit."

In this interchange, the assertive receptionist has stated the two requirements that the customer must fulfill before business can be transacted. Even though the customer is aggressive, the receptionist maintains an assertive style marked by a firm but controlled voice.

Customer: "Who's in charge here?"

Response: "I am."

Customer: "No, I mean of the whole operation. Come on, I want to talk to the top banana."

Response: "My responsibility is to determine who at our company can best help you. For me to do my job, you will have to help me by describing your problem."

The assertive "I am" at the beginning of this conversation established the lines of authority. This customer now knows how to work through the system so that his concerns will be heard.

Customer : (Screaming) "This place is so screwed up, I can't believe it!"

Response: "How can I help you?"

Customer : (Screaming) "Every month for the past six years I have sent you my money and what do I get in return — nothing!"

Response: "How can I help you?"

Customer : (Screaming) "Look at you, you're just like everyone
            else around here — worthless!"
Response: "How can I help you?"

This emotionally distraught customer is looking for a fight.
The assertive receptionist refuses to jump into the ring. Even
when the personal attack was made, the assertive person refuses
to become aggressive.

Firmly repeating the question "How can I help you?" accom-
plishes two goals. First, the question helps the customer focus
his feelings into one action.   Second, by repeating the question,
the customer knows you cannot be baited into a personal fight.

The Telephone Customer

Since you cannot see the customer at the other end of the
telephone line, it is important for the assertive communicator to
develop skills of reading the rhythm and pitch in someone's
voice.

In the statement "just a minute," if each word is said with the
same rhythm and pitch, it is a simple request. If the accent is
placed on "just," annoyance is communicated. If the word
"minute" is emphasized, impatience is the message.

To illustrate the change in meanings, repeat the following
sentences using a different voice inflection to accent certain
words.

- "You're sweet."

- "I guess."

- "I'm sure."

- "In my opinion."

- "I'm not going home with you."

Did you hear the different meanings? When you speak over
the telephone, the only way you communicate, besides the
words, is the rhythm and pitch of your voice.

Knowing that customers will communicate a variety of meanings, here are the steps to follow when you want to assertively respond.

1. Identify the real message. If a customer says, "The directions for putting together your barbeque grill *certainly* were clear," you have received the message that the directions were not clear. Here is a frustrated customer who doesn't know how to say, "I am angry because the directions for assembling my barbeque grill don't give me the information I need." Also notice his initial statement was "...your barbeque grill." Even though he bought this product, he is not sure he wants to own it. An assertive response might be, "Mr. Jones, are the directions for putting together your grill *not* clear?" The emphasis you have placed on "not" gives the customer permission to talk about the real issue.

2. Clarify options. You may want to summarize a telephone conversation with a customer this way, "Mr. Jones, after listening to your concerns, here are the three choices we have... Which one would best satisfy you?" Be careful not to list an option which is impossible or unacceptable to you.

3. Use "I" statements. It is easy to use your company or organization as the scapegoat for your decisions in dealing with a customer over the telephone. "Since your warranty has expired, we cannot help you." The personal pronoun "we" often confuses the customer because he doesn't know who is responsible for deciding if his warranty is void. If you just made that decision, the assertive response should be, "Because your radio is no longer covered under the warranty, I cannot authorize the company to pay for the repairs. I will be happy to supply a list of repair shops in your area."

"I" statements are also an assertive way to conclude a telephone call. "I need to end our conversation now. I've enjoyed talking to you..." is an appropriate way to conclude your interaction with a customer.

The Delinquent Customer

Someone owes you money for a product or service you have supplied. You have sent several written notices to this person during the past few months. There has been no response from the Delinquent Customer.

Most of us avoid a difficult situation like this. We want to be understanding, but the non-responsive attitude of this customer creates confusion and anger.

The assertive communicator must refuse to give in to these feelings. The customer has to participate in the resolution of this issue. The first step is to arrange a personal meeting (if it is feasible).

An assertive statement at this face-to-face meeting might be, "I am confused. On January 16, March 1 and April 30, I sent you notice that your outstanding balance of $300 has not been paid. I need to know if there are extenuating circumstances that make it impossible for you to pay this bill. If not, I need either a check now or a specific date when this balance will be paid."

Assertiveness allows for mistakes and inaction, but assertiveness insists on accountability. Notice that the conversation provides for both understanding and contractual accountability.

Probably the most challenging situation is when the customer is very angry. The following steps should be taken when you come face-to-face with a very angry person.

How to Handle Angry People

1. ***Don't be funny.*** You may use inappropriate humor. This defense mechanism only further enrages the person because he thinks, "This person doesn't know how angry I am!"

2. ***Don't argue.*** Arguing leads nowhere. If you get into a shouting match with an angry person, no one wins.

3. ***Listen.*** This may be the hardest part of dealing with an angry person. Listen attentively for this person's needs. Does he need attention, status, control, etc.? Is there a way you can respond to his need?

4. Use the person's name. When the angry person finally slows down, break in using his name. The sweetest word a listener can hear is his name. If you ever hear a word that even comes close to sounding like your name, watch your response. Did your head turn? Did you stop what you were doing? You will get someone's attention when you use his name.

5. Slow down. Usually when someone is very angry, his speech will be rapid. As you begin to enter into the conversation, slow down your rate of speech as a model for the other person.

6. Lower your voice. Also, as you are speaking, progressively bring down the volume of your voice. Begin speaking at the same intensity, rate and volume as the angry person, but slowly lead the person to a more reasonable tone.

7. Sit down. It is amazing how sitting not only lowers the body, but brings rapid thoughts and words under control. Ask the other person to take a seat as you discuss the issue at hand, and watch how rationality is restored.

8. Negotiate. As discussed in Chapter 5, find ways to confront and integrate.

If this angry person is on the other end of a telephone conversation, use the principles just discussed, but add these unique coping mechanisms:

1. Interrupt the angry person at an acceptable place and ask this question, "Excuse me, if there is one thing I could do to help you right now, what would it be?" This question helps the person focus on the reason for the phone call. Sometimes people just blow up without having a solution in mind. Once this person has been specific, then respond honestly.

2. If the angry person will not slow down or be reasonable, make arrangements with someone else in the office to handle the call. Break in and say, "Mr. Jones, I am not the right

person to help you. Please hold and an associate of mine will handle your complaint." Then make sure the person waits no more than one minute before someone else from your office talks to him. Changing listeners, with a short interlude, provides the angry person with "down time" to reconsider how he wants to communicate his message.

3. Arrange a personal meeting. Since you do not have the advantage of reading body language over the telephone, you may want to have this person meet with you.

4. Never hang up. When you hang up you only make the person angrier. If you need to conclude the call, arrange for either yourself or someone else to call him back at a later time.

For Your Review

Customers are special people. They ultimately decide whether your product or service should exist. Every time you gain and keep a customer, another vote is cast for or against your product or service.

We learned that customers may not always be right, but they should be satisfied. Assertiveness can guarantee customer satisfaction and preserve your rights.

Review this chapter by deciding your assertive responses to these five encounters with customers:

1. There is an angry customer on the phone who keeps scream-ing and repeating himself.

2. A customer, who you have serviced over a long period of time, complains about the quality of your company's work.

3. You are the community coordinator for the Red Cross. A volunteer has just come into your office to announce her resignation in the middle of the annual fund drive.

4. A customer screams across your reception desk, "I think you and this whole company are trying to rip off this community."

5. You are a professional tax preparer. One of your customers has not paid his bill from last year's tax preparation. You meet this person on the street.

9

TEACHING OTHERS TO COMMUNICATE ASSERTIVELY

After reading this book, not only can you improve your assertive communication skills, but you can model new behavior for those around you. As co-workers, family members and friends see the new, assertive you, they will respond differently. You may encounter attempts at manipulation.

Your assertive skills may create some initial confusion. Don't panic. If you are comfortable with the changes you are making, it really doesn't matter what others think.

Throughout this final chapter, you will find specific assertive skills that others can copy with your encouragement. After you have used one of these skills, you may want to say (if the listener appears receptive to advice), "I have illustrated an assertive skill you may want to use. Let me go over exactly what I was thinking and how I expressed myself. Please give me your reaction."

As you take time to teach, by example, assertive communication skills to people you know and trust, your future relationships with these "students" will move from manipulation to assertion.

Here are some of the major assertiveness skills you should use regularly.

Fogging

Dr. Manuel J. Smith, in his bestselling book, *When I Say No, I Feel Guilty*, describes the technique of fogging.

Dr. Smith uses the term fogging because the characteristics of this assertive skill are similar to observing a fog bank while standing on a beach. The fog bank obscures the view without offering resistance.

Using this analogy, fogging is the practice of resisting manipulation without giving the other person an opportunity to direct a counter-attack. In principle, fogging can take the form of:

1. Agreeing with any truth in the manipulation.

2. Agreeing with any possibility of truth in the manipulation.

3. Agreeing with general truths in logical statements.

Let's demonstrate fogging in the following dialogue between Sue and her supervisor, Jane.

Jane: "Well, your monthly report certainly is as short as usual."

Sue: "Yes, my monthly report is brief." (Fogging)

What did you read into Jane's comment? What is the real message she is giving Sue? Obviously, Jane is a passive person who finds it difficult to talk about the unacceptable brevity of Sue's monthly reports, so she makes Sue feel guilty by being sarcastic.

Sue decided not to be manipulated. Her fogging deals with the facts, not the guilt or sarcasm. Let's look at the same setting, only this time Jane will be aggressive.

Jane: (Screaming) "I can't believe the length of this monthly report. I have a grocery list in my purse longer than this thing."

Sue: "Yes, I try to keep my monthly reports brief." (Fogging)

Sue refuses to be intimidated by Jane's attack. Jane has nowhere to go with her observation on the brevity of Sue's reports — unless she wants to be assertive and say what she is really thinking. Fogging does two things:

1. It forces the manipulator to focus on the real issue. Jane has to deal with the length of the report. Fogging makes both parties look at the real issue.

2. It forces the manipulator to think of other possibilities. Maybe this aggressive manipulation will not work. Fogging forces Jane to try some other method of getting her message to Sue.

Negative Assertion

When we make errors, people sometimes seize those moments to hold our feet to the fire. Maybe there are co-workers who wait for you to make a mistake. When you do, these people let you and the rest of the world know.

If you would like an assertive response which takes the wind out of their sails, you may want to use negative assertion.

Negative assertion involves not only agreeing with your adversary, but using exaggeration to further emphasize that you were wrong. Here is a conversation between John and his co-worker, Sam. Sam has discovered an error in John's mathematical calculations on a bid for a construction project.

Sam: "I can't believe it — another one. John, you have made four mistakes in this Acme bid. What's the matter, aren't you playing with a full deck?"

John: "Sam, you are right again. I keep making the same mistakes. I'm so glad you picked up on those errors. What is wrong with me?" (Negative Assertion)

The assumption behind negative assertion is that the criticism is legitimate.

Negative Inquiry

Let's turn the tables. What if the criticism doesn't have any factual basis? What if someone manipulates you with false guilt by making a judgment which, in your opinion, is not true?

Along with fogging, which is a simple statement of agreement, you can try another assertive skill called negative inquiry. Instead of being confrontational, you ask your opponent to elaborate on why you are wrong.

Let's look at an interaction between Kathy and Jack, the president of an advertising agency. Jack walks into Kathy's office and throws down some of her sketches for an ad campaign.

Jack: "You call this art work. I have never seen anything so pathetic from this department."

Kathy: "What makes this art work so pathetic?" (Negative Inquiry)

Jack: "Well...well...just look at this page. I mean, after all, where is someone supposed to start reading the copy?"

Kathy: "I'm confused. You obviously read the copy. Specifically, why is this page so difficult to read?" (Negative Inquiry)

Jack: "Well, I started right here. But I don't know who else would have known to begin here."

Kathy: "Specifically what changes should I make to this layout?" (Negative Inquiry)

Negative inquiry does not confront the other person in a
defensive way. With this skill, you continue to ask the person to
define the specific issues. The result of this process is to identify areas where you need improvement. You've also taught
someone how to deal with you constructively.

Broken Record

There are times we give an assertive response to manipulation and people just can't believe what they hear. They continue
to try guilt, power, embarrassment, seduction and a host of other
manipulative tools even after we have been open and honest.

Since an assertive person doesn't have to apologize for his
thoughts and feelings, there is no reason to give in just because
someone continues to manipulate.

One of the best ways to end a manipulative conversation is to
try the Broken Record technique. Once you have given your
assertive response, continue to repeat yourself even if the manipulator's tactics change.

Bob, the office manager, is having a discussion with Trish, a
secretary.

Bob: "Trish, I want that Holmes report done two days early."

Trish: "With all the other deadlines I have, I cannot finish the
Holmes report two days early. What projects can be
postponed so I can get the report done?" (Broken
Record)

Bob: "Look, I've seen you over there reading *The National
Enquirer* and painting your nails. There is no reason you
can't work a little harder and get this report done."

Trish: "With all the other deadlines I have, I cannot finish the
Holmes report two days early. What projects can be
postponed so I can get the report done?" (Broken
Record)

Bob: "If you don't get it to me when I want it, the President is going to be angry at the two of us."

Trish: "With all the other deadlines I have, I cannot finish the Holmes report two days early. What projects can be postponed so I can get the report done?" (Broken Record)

Bob tried three different approaches to manipulate Trish into getting what he wants. First, it was the power play of, "I'm-the-boss-you're-the-peon." Second, Bob tried the guilt trip with comments about reading and painting nails. Third, Bob tried to intimidate by dropping the title of a higher authority.

Trish was not insubordinate, just honest. The Broken Record technique should lead to negotiation so the Holmes report is done on time.

Squeaky Wheel Technique

This skill is especially effective for the supervisor or manager. If you have a passive worker who uses avoidance as a way to protect himself from the pain of confrontation, you may want to use the Squeaky Wheel technique.

Very simply, you communicate a clear message to the avoider and then *leave*. Your natural inclination will be to push this person until he responds. In effect, you may reinforce the avoidance because the issue becomes the confrontation, not what you want done.

Larry approaches Dennis, who is working on a budget request memo. Dennis obviously has a very bad case of "writer's block." Larry has observed Dennis staring at his typewriter for the past hour.

Larry: "Is the budget request memo finished?"

Dennis: "I...I will have it for you soon."

Larry: "I will be back in 10 minutes to pick it up."

Larry knows that the memo has not been started. He also knows that in 10 minutes the memo will still not be finished. In 10 minutes, Larry will come back and say, "I'm here for the budget request memo."

If the memo is still not ready, Larry will simply say, "I will be back in an hour to pick it up. The memo must be finished by that time."

It would have been much easier to threaten Dennis with ultimatums. But Dennis will never learn how to work with Larry unless Larry lets Dennis know what is expected without manipulation.

Assumed Agreement

Another way to teach avoidant people to communicate openly is to use Assumed Agreement.

The most difficult thing for most people to do is make decisions. Avoidant people procrastinate about decisions. The problem with making decisions is that you never have all the information required to make the perfect decision. Perfectionists are usually terrible decision-makers because they keep waiting for more data before deciding.

You can teach an avoidant person to make decisions by saying, "If I do not hear from you by 5 p.m. next Tuesday, I will assume you have given me a 'yes' response. Your response will be presented at next Wednesday's staff meeting."

The avoider may defer to your plan until he is misrepresented before a group of people.

Assertive Responses to Negativity

Here are the responses of an assertive communicator to common negative expressions from people who try to block your assertiveness.

"We can't. It's impossible."

The best assertive response to this comment is, "What prevents us from..."

This helps the negative person focus on the real or perceived problems. It also clarifies the problem and what needs to be done to eliminate it.

"No one...Always...Never...All."

Respond to absolute terms with parroting, "No one?" "Always?" "Never?" "All?"   When you respond with a question, you force the other person to find the exception to these terms.

For example, Linda walks into your office and says, "No one cares what happens to this account." You can say, "No one cares? Do you mean there isn't one person in this entire office that genuinely cares about these people who have been our customers for the last 20 years?"

The fallacy of Linda's statement will be clear to her and you.

"You are wrong."

The assertive response to this accusatory statement is, "What evidence do you have that I am wrong?" This is a negative inquiry that requires the accuser to pinpoint the specific reason for his accusation.

For Your Review

If you want to share the insights you have learned about assertiveness, the best way is to continuously model assertive skills. This chapter has summarized some of the basic skills you need to master in assertive communication.

Answer the following questions to see how well you have learned the basics of assertive behavior.

1. Late yesterday afternoon, someone in the office came up to you and said, "You're wrong." What is your response?

2. If you answered a co-worker's criticism of your work with, "Yes, you are right. I did place the order too late." Which assertive skill would you be using?

   a. Fogging.

   b. Negative Assertion.

   c. Negative Inquiry.

   d. Fogging and Negative Assertion.

3. There is a heated debate in a staff meeting. Someone looks at you and says, "We can't do this." What is your response?

4. In a meeting with a supervisor you say, "What is there about my work that makes it unacceptable?" Which technique in this chapter would you be using?

   a. Fogging.

   b. Negative Assertion.

   c. Negative Inquiry.

   d. None of the above.

5. When you firmly respond with the same words over and over, what assertive skill are you using?

Suggested Reading

Alberti, Robert E. and Emmons, Michael L. *Your Perfect Right.* San Luis Obispo, CA: Impact Publishers, 1986.

Andersen, Richard. *Writing That Works.* New York, NY: McGraw-Hill Publishing, 1989.

Bramson, Robert M. *Coping With Difficult People.* Garden City, NY: Anchor Press, 1981.

Burley-Allen, Madelyn. *Managing Assertively.* New York, NY: John Wiley & Sons, 1983.

Carr-Ruffino, Norma. *The Promotable Woman.* Belmont, CA: Wadsworth Publishing, 1985.

Forsyth, Robert D. *Getting It Together.* Springfield, MO: Reflex Management Publishing, 1986.

Robinson, James W. *Winning Them Over.* Rocklin, CA: Prima Publishing, 1987.

Rosen, Leonard. *The Everyday English Handbook.* New York, NY: Dell Publishing, 1985.

Smith, Manuel J. *When I Say No, I Feel Guilty.* New York, NY: Bantam Books, 1975.

INDEX

NOTES

NOTES

Buy two, get one free!

Each of our handbook series (LIFESTYLE, COMMUNICATION, PRODUCTIVITY, and LEADERSHIP) was designed to give you the most comprehensive collection of hands-on desktop references related to a specific topic. These handbooks are a great value at the regular price of $12.95 ($14.95 in Canada); plus, at the unbeatable offer of buy two at the regular price and get one free, you can't find a better value in learning resources. **To order**, see the back of this page for the entire handbook selection.

1. Fill out and send the entire page by mail to:

    National Press Publications
    6901 West 63rd Street
    P.O. Box 2949
    Shawnee Mission, Kansas 66201-1349

2. Or **FAX 1-913-432-0824**

3. Or call toll-free **1-800-258-7248** (**1-800-685-4142** in Canada)

Fill out completely:

Name _____

Organization _____

Address _____

City _____

State/Province _____ ZIP/Postal Code _____

Telephone ( ) _____

Method of Payment:

❑ Enclosed is my check or money order

❑ Please charge to:

    ❑ MasterCard   ❑ VISA   ❑ American Express

Signature _____ Exp. Date _____

Credit Card Number

❑ ❑ ❑ ❑ ❑ ❑ ❑ ❑ ❑ ❑ ❑ ❑

To order multiple copies for co-workers and friends: U.S. Can.

	U.S.	Can.
20-50 copies	$8.50	$10.95
More than 50 copies	$7.50	$9.95

VIP# 705-008442-092

OTHER DESKTOP HANDBOOKS

	Qty	Item#	Title	U.S.	Can.	Total
LEADERSHIP		410	The Supervisor's Handbook	$12.95	$14.95	
		418	Total Quality Management	$12.95	$14.95	
		421	Change: Coping with Tomorrow Today	$12.95	$14.95	
		459	Techniques of Successful Delegation	$12.95	$14.95	
		463	Powerful Leadership Skills for Women	$12.95	$14.95	
		494	Team-Building	$12.95	$14.95	
		495	How to Manage Conflict	$12.95	$14.95	
		469	Peak Performance	$12.95	$14.95	
COMMUNICATION		413	Dynamic Communication Skills for Women	$12.95	$14.95	
		414	The Write Stuff: *A Style Manual for Effective Business Writing*	$12.95	$14.95	
		417	Listen Up: *Hear What's Really Being Said*	$12.95	$14.95	
		442	Assertiveness: *Get What You Want Without Being Pushy*	$12.95	$14.95	
		460	Techniques to Improve Your Writing Skills	$12.95	$14.95	
		461	Powerful Presentation Skills	$12.95	$14.95	
		482	Techniques of Effective Telephone Communication	$12.95	$14.95	
		485	Personal Negotiating Skills	$12.95	$14.95	
		488	Customer Service: *The Key to Winning Lifetime Customers*	$12.95	$14.95	
		498	How to Manage Your Boss	$12.95	$14.95	
PRODUCTIVITY		411	Getting Things Done: *An Achiever's Guide to Time Management*	$12.95	$14.95	
		443	A New Attitude	$12.95	$14.95	
		468	Understanding the Bottom Line: *Finance for the Non-Financial Manager*	$12.95	$14.95	
		483	Successful Sales Strategies: *A Woman's Perspective*	$12.95	$14.95	
		489	Doing Business Over the Phone: *Telemarketing for the '90s*	$12.95	$14.95	
		496	Motivation & Goal-Setting: *The Keys to Achieving Success*	$12.95	$14.95	
LIFESTYLE		415	Balancing Career & Family: *Overcoming the Superwoman Syndrome*	$12.95	$14.95	
		416	Real Men Don't Vacuum	$12.95	$14.95	
		464	Self-Esteem: *The Power to Be Your Best*	$12.95	$14.95	
		484	The Stress Management Handbook	$12.95	$14.95	
		486	Parenting: *Ward & June Don't Live Here Anymore*	$12.95	$14.95	
		487	How to Get the Job You Want	$12.95	$14.95	

SALES TAX
All purchases subject to state and local sales tax.
Questions? Call
1-800-258-7248

Subtotal	
Sales Tax (Add appropriate state and local tax)	
Shipping and Handling ($1 one item; 50¢ each additional item)	
Total	

VIP# 705-008442-092